Contents

4

I feel ill

I feel ill when I wake up. I am too hot and Mum says that I have a **temperature**.

Mum phones the doctor and makes an **appointment**.

It is my first time going to the doctor. I am a bit worried, but Mum says it will be fine.

The waiting room

When we get to the doctor's we see the receptionist. We tell her we have an appointment.

We have to wait in the waiting room until the doctor can see me.

The receptionist says we won't have to wait long.

The doctor

When it is my turn to see the doctor, mum comes with me.

The doctor says hello and tells me her name.

She asks me to sit down.

9

The doctor asks what
is wrong with me.
Mum talks to her.

The doctor tells me to
stick out my tongue.
I open my mouth wide
and she looks at
my throat.

"Now I will check your temperature," she says. "I need to see if you have a **fever**."

The doctor uses a **stethoscope** to listen to my chest and back. She can hear my heart and lungs.

The stethoscope feels cold on my skin.

13

14

The doctor uses a tool
to shine a bright light
into my ear.

She looks into my ear.
It doesn't hurt.

The doctor asks questions about how I feel.

She says I'll be fine but that I need some medicine.

She gives Mum a piece of paper showing the name of the medicine I need.

It is called a **prescription.**

17

Medicine to help

The doctor smiles at me.

"Get lots of sleep and take your medicine," she says. "You will soon feel better."

On our way home, we stop at a chemist to get my medicine.

The bottle has my name on it. It tells us how I have to take the medicine.

MED

One spo

every m

At home, I put on my pyjamas and get into bed.

Mum gives me a spoon
of the medicine. It tastes
funny. I swallow it.

In bed, I think about
my trip to the doctor.

She was kind and
she makes children
feel better.

I think I would like to be a
doctor when I grow up.

Glossary

appointment   a time booked to see the doctor

fever   when you are too hot because you are ill

prescription   a piece of paper from the doctor that lists medicine

stethoscope   a tool to listen to noises inside the body

temperature   when you are ill and your head feels hot